INTRODUCTION

A tropical rain forest is an area of tall trees where it is always warm and it rains almost every day. Within every tropical rain forest you can find an amazing number of different kinds of insects, birds, reptiles, amphibians, fish, and mammals. In fact, more species of plants and animals live in tropical rain forests than in any other place on Earth!

All tropical rain forests are found in the hot, humid areas around the equator. But did you know that not all rain forests are tropical rain forests? Some are temperate rain forests. They are found in parts of the United States, Canada, Europe, and elsewhere.

This book tells you all about tropical rain forests. You'll find out that—

- it's almost always dark in a rain forest
- rain forests are not jungles
- some frogs "fly" from tree to tree
- certain plants catch and eat bugs and frogs
- sometimes fish swim among the tree branches

—and much, much more!

Melvin Berger   Gilda Berger

WET AND HOT

Does it always rain in the rain forest?

Yes. You can count on some rain just about every afternoon in a tropical rain forest. Often, the rainfall is very hard, but it usually lasts less than an hour. At least 6 feet (2 m) of rain falls every year. Many tropical rain forests, however, get far more rain than that. The yearly average is about 21 feet (6.4 m). Compare that with an average of only 3 feet (1 m) a year for the rest of the planet!

What happens to the rain after it falls?

Most is soaked up by tree roots. The water then goes up into the leaves, where it is given off as water vapor. The water vapor goes into the air and forms clouds. In time, the clouds grow too heavy and the water falls as rain in the rain forest and elsewhere. The continuing change from rain, to water vapor, to clouds, and back to rain is called the water cycle.

Why are rain forests called "the lungs of the world"?

Because the millions of trees in the rain forest take in carbon dioxide from the air and give off oxygen. Humans and most animals need oxygen to breathe. The trees of the rain forests provide much of the world's oxygen supply.

Is it always hot in the rain forest?

Yes. It is about 80° Fahrenheit (26.6° C) all year. In fact, there is less difference in temperature between summer and winter than between day and night!

The green areas on the map represent the tropical rain forests of the world.

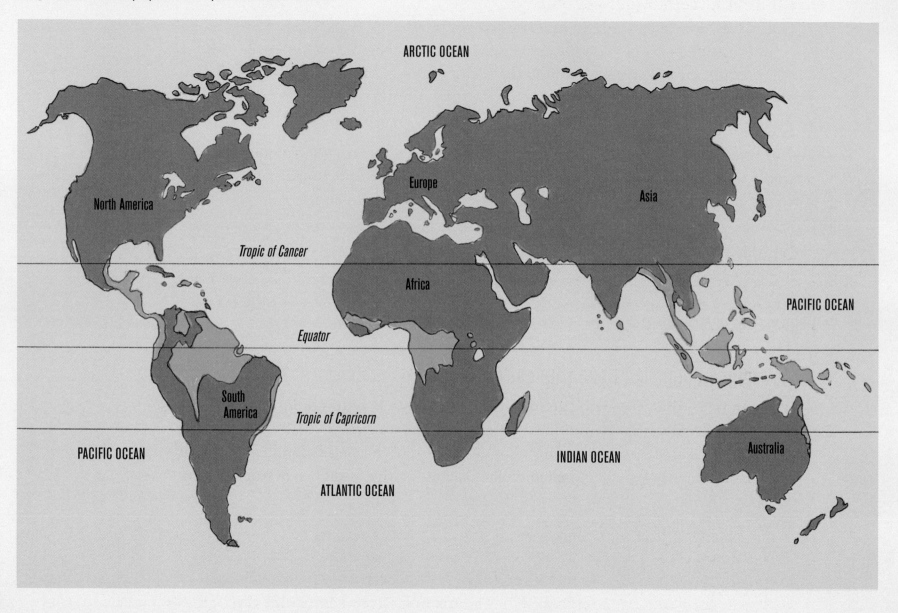

Are rain forests bright and sunny?

Not at all. Very little sunlight reaches the ground because the leaves of the trees in the rain forest block it out. Scientists estimate that less than 1 percent of the sun's light gets to the rain forest floor, making the inside of a rain forest dark and shadowy.

Are rain forests jungles?

No. Jungles have a much thicker and more tangled undergrowth. Compared to a jungle, the floor of a rain forest is clear and open. You might be able to ride your bicycle through parts of a tropical rain forest—but never through a jungle!

Where are tropical rain forests?

Most are found around the equator, between the Tropic of Cancer and the Tropic of Capricorn. Here, the sun shines 12 hours a day. Also, the sun is almost directly overhead at noon, which causes high temperatures.

How many countries have tropical rain forests?

More than 50. But over half the total rain forest area is found in just three countries: Brazil, the Democratic Republic of Congo, and Indonesia.

Altogether, rain forests cover only about 7 percent of the world's land. Although this is a small area, more than half of all animal and plant species in the world live in tropical rain forests!

Where is the world's largest rain forest?

In South America. Called the Amazon rain forest, it covers about one-third of the entire continent. From the air, the forest looks like a vast green carpet covering some 2 million square miles (5.2 million km²). The Amazon River, which runs through this giant rain forest, carries much of the excess rainfall into the Atlantic Ocean.

What are the three layers of the rain forest?

Canopy, understory, and forest floor. Each layer provides a different kind of home to the plants and animals that live there.

The thick, high branches of the tall trees form the sunny, umbrella-like canopy over most of the forest. The tallest trees range from 115 to 150 feet (35 to 46 m) above the ground. More plants and animals live in the canopy than in any other part of the rain forest.

Below the canopy are smaller trees, shrubs, and plants that grow to about 65 feet (20 m). They make up the understory. Little sunlight reaches this middle layer, yet it, too, is full of life.

At the bottom of the rain forest is the dark forest floor, where you find a scattering of seedlings, ferns, and other foliage. Numerous animals, from ants to elephants, live on the ground level.

Do any trees grow above the canopy?

Yes. Giant trees called emergents tower over the canopy. Some emergents rise up more than 250 feet (76 m) above the forest floor. Most have tall, slender trunks, small leaves, and rounded, umbrella-like crowns. A single giant emergent crown can spread out over an acre (hectare) of the rain forest. Each tree releases some 200 gallons (760 l) of water vapor into the atmosphere every day!

Is rain forest soil fertile?

No. Even though millions of giant trees and other plants grow in rain forests, only the thin, top layer of the soil contains nutrients, the chemicals that plants need to grow.

In rain forests, trees, plants, and animals die and fall to the ground. The high heat and humidity help insects and bacteria quickly break down the debris into nutrients. But the heavy rainfall washes away most of the nutrients, leaving the soil food-poor. Considering the infertile soil, the diversity of plants in a tropical rain forest is truly amazing!

PLANT LIFE

How many different kinds of trees grow in a tropical rain forest?

Tens of thousands! Unlike other forests, the rain forest has many different tree species per acre (hectare)—but only a few of each kind of tree. To take one example: More species of trees (835, to be exact) grow in 125 acres (50 ha) of tropical forest in Malaysia than in all of the United States!

Why are there so many different species in the rain forest?

Because the sunlight, rainfall, and temperature vary from area to area and from layer to layer. Many species grow only where the conditions are right. But there is only enough space in each area for a limited number of plants and animals. So just a few individuals of any one species live in each part of the rain forest.

Do rain forest trees have deep roots?

No. Most tree roots grow close to the surface. This lets them quickly absorb the nutrients that are found in the top layer of the soil. But shallow roots do not support trees as well as deep roots do.

What keeps rain forest trees from blowing over?

Huge growths on the trunks called buttresses. These triangular supports help hold up the trees by spreading their weight out over broad areas.

   Smaller trees sometimes have long, polelike structures, called stilts, growing from their trunks. These also keep the trees upright.

Buttresses

Stilts

Brazil nut flowers

Strangler fig
around host tree

Does the rain forest keep changing?

Yes. Left to itself, the rain forest changes slowly. From time to time, a tall old tree dies and falls to the ground, leaving a large gap in the canopy. The sun is then able to reach the small trees growing in the shade of the understory. As sunshine floods in, these trees spurt up and fill the gap in the canopy.

What tree kills other trees?

The strangler fig tree. Birds, bats, and other animals eat the fruit of this tree and drop the small seeds onto the branches of another tree, called the host. A seed starts to grow high up in the host tree. Slowly, the roots reach down to the ground and take hold in the soil.

In time, the fig tree grows into a full-sized tree around the host tree. But true to its name, the strangler fig tree chokes the life out of its host—and sometimes nearby trees, too. No wonder Spanish-speaking people call this tree *matapalo*, or "tree killer"!

How do Brazil nut trees grow?

With two animal helpers. The first is the euglossine (you-GLAH-seen), a shiny green bee that sips nectar from the fluffy white flowers of the Brazil nut tree. When the bee flies from flower to flower, pollen grains that stick to its body fall off. The pollen fertilizes the flowers, which develop into seed pods. Each pod contains as many as 24 separate Brazil nuts. When ripe, the pod falls to the ground.

The agouti (uh-GOO-tee) is a small rodent that feeds on seeds. With its sharp teeth, the animal breaks open the fallen pods and the nuts. Often, it buries half-chewed, soggy nuts in the ground. Some of the nuts take root and grow into new Brazil nut trees. It sounds nuts, but these trees won't grow without their animal helpers!

What do we get from the kapok tree?

Many things. From the seedpods we get a waterproof fiber called kapok. This soft material makes an ideal stuffing for life jackets and mattresses. The kapok tree also produces an oil that people use in cattle feed and to make soap. People living in the rain forest make canoes and rafts from the wood of the kapok tree.

Do rain forest trees lose their leaves?

Yes. Most trees are always losing some old leaves and growing new ones. Only a few species drop all of their leaves for a short time at certain seasons.

Do tree leaves soak up rainwater?

Some do. But many trees have long leaves with pointed ends, called drip tips. The rainwater drips off the leaves so they dry quickly.

Other trees have smooth, waxy leaves, which help them get rid of excess water. This shiny surface stops moss and mold from growing on the leaves. Without moss or mold blocking the light, the leaves are better able to use sunlight to make food.

Which rain forest tree has the biggest leaves in the world?

A palm tree known as Raphia taedigera (RAH-fee-uh tuh-DIJ-er-uh). The leaves, or fronds, of this short, stout tree can be 70 feet (21 m) long and 19 feet (6 m) wide. Each one can reach up to the top of a seven-story building and halfway across a tennis court!

Kapok tree

Bromeliad pool

Which plants have their roots in the air?

Epiphytes (EP-uh-fites). These plants grow on the branches and trunks of tall trees in the canopy where they get lots of sunlight. Some collect pools of rain in their leaves and get nutrients from plant and animal debris. Others drop roots down to the forest floor and pick up water and nutrients that way. Still others thrive on the humidity and floating bits of dust in the air.

What is the best-known epiphyte?

The bromeliad (bro-MEE-lee-add). Built something like the top of a pineapple, this plant has a large, hollow center that can hold as much as 12 gallons (45 l) of rainwater. Look into a bromeliad pool and you'll be surprised at what you see: snails, beetles, salamanders laying eggs, and tree frogs with their tadpoles!

The bromeliad gets nutrients from the wastes of the animals that live in the water. It is also fed by the remains of other plants that fall into the rainwater pool.

Which plant catches insects?

The pitcher plant. Its leaves are vase-shaped and filled with a sweet liquid that lures insects inside. Once the insects slip into the liquid, they can't get out. The liquid dissolves the bugs, providing the plant with the nutrients it needs. If small frogs don't look where they're going, they may also fall into this plant trap!

What is the world's largest flower?

The rafflesia (ra-FLEE-zhuh). This giant red flower grows on the roots or stems of shrubs in the Malaysian rain forest. The biggest rafflesia reaches the staggering size of 3 feet (1 m) across and weighs 13 pounds (6 kg)!

The rafflesia also takes the prize for being the ugliest and worst-smelling of all flowers. Still, the stench attracts insects—and they help to spread the rafflesia seeds.

How do vines grow in the rain forest?

Some sprout on the forest floor and creep up trees toward the sunny canopy. They grip the trees' bark with special hooks or tendrils. Other vines start from seeds that fall onto trees in the canopy. These drop their roots down to the forest floor and then start to grow.

Which vines are the biggest?

Lianas (lee-AH-nuhz). These huge, woody vines can be up to 800 feet (244 m) long and as thick as a man's body! Lianas may start in the ground, grow up to the top of one tree, and loop down to the ground again. Many twist around and around trees in the canopy like ropes, tying them together. Watch out! If one tree in the forest falls, it often pulls others down with it!

What is the fastest growing grass in the rain forest?

Bamboo. Some bamboo shoots up at the rate of 24 inches (61 cm) in 24 hours. Bamboo as tall as a child one day can be the height of a grown-up the next day!

What water plant can you stand on?

The Amazonian Victoria water lily. Its leaves are up to 6 feet (2 m) wide. They're strong enough to hold you up above the water!

Jacana

Lianas

Amazonian Victoria
water lily pads and flowers

19

Brazil nut tree

Cacao tree

Sapodilla tree

What is the most common rain forest plant product?

Wood. Millions of trees are harvested from rain forests every year. Most are used for firewood. But some kinds of wood are too valuable to burn. Because they are beautiful, strong, and long-lasting, these tropical woods have many uses. Mahogany is used for furniture and wall panels. Ebony is used for black piano keys, golf clubs, and some musical instruments. Teak is used for boats and furniture. Very light balsa wood is used to make model airplanes and life rafts.

Why is the rain forest sometimes called "the nursery of the world"?

Because most of today's foods originated in a rain forest. This includes sugar, rice, corn, bananas, coconuts, coffee and tea, pepper and other spices, vanilla and other flavorings, and cacao beans for making chocolate.

And then there's chicle from the sapodilla tree in Central America. While hardly a food, chicle is used to make chewing gum.

Which houseplants grow in rain forests?

Many, including African violets, orchids, palms, and bromeliads. The use of tropical rain forest plants in the home dates back to about 2000 B.C.!

How many medicines come from rain forest plants?

About one out of every four. The estimated value of these drugs is over $50 billion a year.

Many tropical plants contain ingredients that have been used to make antibiotics, painkillers, and heart drugs. The U.S. National Cancer Institute has found thousands of plants with anti-cancer properties—and 7 out of every 10 come from the rain forest! The rosy periwinkle, for instance, produces a substance used to treat leukemia and other forms of cancer. Other plants work against different diseases, from malaria to high blood pressure.

ANIMAL LIFE

Which animals live in the rain forest?

About half of all animal species on Earth! A patch of rain forest measuring 4 square miles (10 km²) contains perhaps 125 mammal species, 400 bird species, 100 reptile species, 60 amphibian species, and about 40,000 different kinds of insects. Nowhere else in the world can you find as many different species as you can in the rain forest.

How do most animals keep in touch?

With sound. In the canopy, understory, or on the forest floor, members of the same species can have difficulty communicating. Animal populations are usually small and scattered about. And the dense leaves and dim light of the forest make it hard for them to see one another. So instead of sight, most animals use sound to keep in touch. The rain forest resounds with the calls of monkeys, birds, insects, and frogs trying to attract mates or warn away enemies.

Which is the noisiest animal in the canopy?

The howler monkey. You can usually hear its booming calls, HUH! HUH! HUH!, on cool mornings when sound travels farthest. The sounds can be heard from as far away as 2 miles (3 km).

Howler monkeys, like many monkeys of the rain forests in Central and South America, drop partly eaten fruits and flowers to the ground. This spreads seeds and provides food for animals on the ground.

The monkeys also help trees by ripping off heavy epiphytes as they hunt for grubs and other edible insects or animals.

Howler monkey

Borneo orangutan

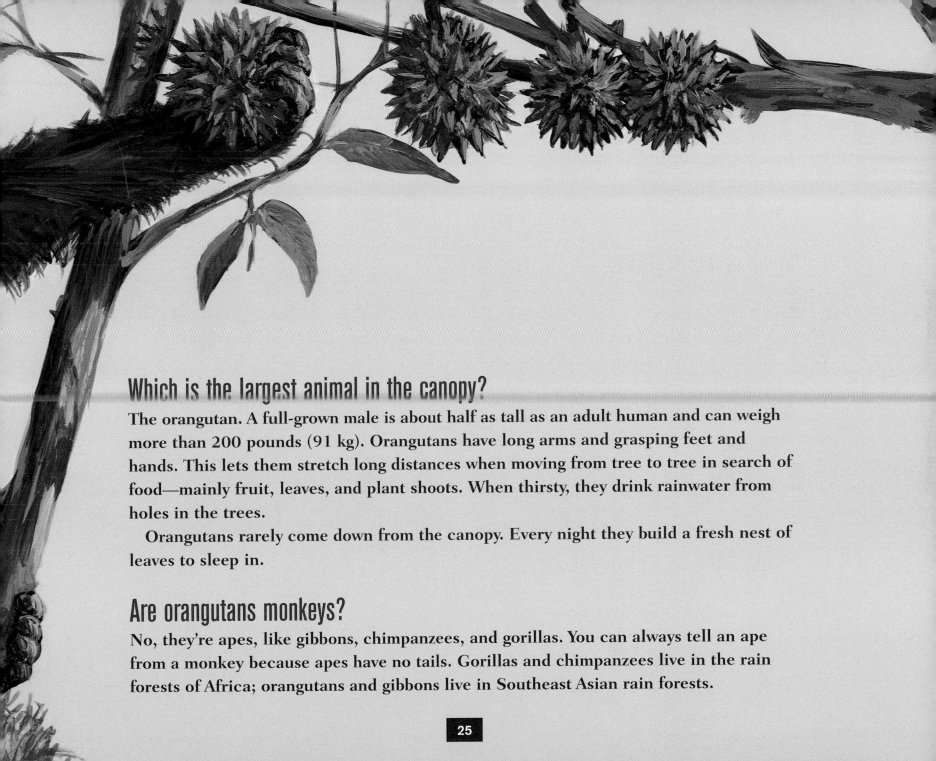

Which is the largest animal in the canopy?

The orangutan. A full-grown male is about half as tall as an adult human and can weigh more than 200 pounds (91 kg). Orangutans have long arms and grasping feet and hands. This lets them stretch long distances when moving from tree to tree in search of food—mainly fruit, leaves, and plant shoots. When thirsty, they drink rainwater from holes in the trees.

Orangutans rarely come down from the canopy. Every night they build a fresh nest of leaves to sleep in.

Are orangutans monkeys?

No, they're apes, like gibbons, chimpanzees, and gorillas. You can always tell an ape from a monkey because apes have no tails. Gorillas and chimpanzees live in the rain forests of Africa; orangutans and gibbons live in Southeast Asian rain forests.

Which birds live in the rain forest canopy?

One out of every three bird species—some 2,600 species in all. The birds are very important because they drop seeds that grow into new plants.

Parrots and toucans are two brightly colored species that nest and feed in the trees. They seldom come to the ground. Parrots use their powerful bills to crack hard nuts and seeds. Toucans snip off figs and other soft fruits with the sawlike edges of their large bills.

Which is the largest bird in the rain forest?

The harpy eagle. Males can weigh over 20 pounds (9 kg) and stand 3½ feet (1 m) tall. Their prey consists of monkeys, sloths, and opossums, which they swoop down and grab with their hand-sized talons. In South America, harpy eagles chase howler monkeys through the leafy canopy at a top speed of 50 miles an hour (80 kph)!

Which birds can fly like helicopters?

Hummingbirds. The birds fly backward and forward, or hover in place while drinking nectar from vine flowers. Hummingbirds can lift off on the spot by flapping their wings up to 50 times a second. They take their name from the sound their wings make when they fly.

Do any birds fly, climb, and swim?

Yes. Hoatzins (hoh-AHT-sins) can fly like most other birds. But their young have claws on their wings so they can also climb up tree trunks. They can swim, too.

Usually, hoatzins feed on the leaves of trees near streams. When a young hoatzin is threatened, it dives down into the water until the danger passes. Then it swims to shore, climbs up the tree, and returns to its meal.

Adult hoatzin

Young hoatzins

Tent-building bats

Fruit-eating bat
carrying a piper fruit

Free-tailed bat

Hawk moth

Do any birds migrate to the rain forest?

Yes. About one out of every three kinds of birds from cold areas migrates to rain forests for the winter. This includes some birds that you may know very well. Among the most familiar species that fly to the tropics every year are warblers, tanagers, thrushes, and orioles.

Are there dragons in the rain forest?

No. The animal we call a flying dragon is really a lizard. It spreads its skin into wings and glides from tree to tree in the canopy or understory. The flying frog of Java glides through the air in much the same way, using its large webbed feet as parachutes.

Which understory mammals fly at night?

Bats. In tropical rain forests, bats make up more than half of all mammal species. Most bats are insect eaters. One kind, the slit faced bat, eats as many as 3,000 insects in a single night.

Other bats are nectar and fruit eaters. As the Marianas fruit bat feeds, it picks up pollen that it spreads to other plants. It also eats the pulp and drops the seeds of various fruits. Up to 95 percent of the trees in cleared areas of the rain forest grow from seeds spread by fruit-eating bats!

Why do most bats feed at night?

For many reasons. For one thing, it's cooler at night. Scientists think that bats and some other animals that feed at night may prefer the cooler temperature. Also, at night, fewer animals are competing for the same food. And finally, it's usually easier for bats to escape from predators in the dark than by the light of day.

Which animals live on the rain forest floor?

Mostly plant eaters. In African rain forests, giant forest hogs weighing 600 pounds (300 kg) travel in herds of about 20. The hogs eat the leaves of low-growing shrubs.

In Southeast Asia, black-and-white tapirs (TAY-puhrs) browse along riverbanks, munching on grass, buds, twigs, and fruit. They are good swimmers and can often be found in the river eating water plants and keeping cool.

Do any birds live on the rain forest floor?

Yes. Pheasants, peacocks, peafowls, and flightless cassowaries (KAS-uh-wer-eez) spend most of their time walking around on the ground. Their diet consists of berries, fruits, seeds, and insects. One forest floor bird, the jungle fowl, is the ancestor of the domestic chicken.

Which rain forest animal does not have teeth?

The anteater. A long, thin snout holds its sticky, pink tongue. The anteater breaks open ant and termite nests with its sharp claws. Then it flicks out its tongue to capture the fleeing insects.

Which animal has the longest tongue?

The okapi (oh-KAH-pee). This relative of the giraffe has a 14-inch (36 cm) black tongue that curls around the leaves it eats. The okapi's tongue is long enough to clean its ears!

What are the largest rodents in the world?

Capybaras (kap-uh-BAHR-uhz). These relatives of mice and squirrels are about the size of German shepherds or other large dogs.

Capybaras live in groups near rivers in the rain forest. They graze on long grasses and moist water lilies. Called "water pigs," capybaras can stay underwater for up to 10 minutes at a time.

Okapi

Congo peafowl

Which is the most feared animal in the rain forest?

The jaguar. Like other big cats, jaguars are fast-running meat eaters that are also good at climbing trees. The animals usually pursue prey alone at night.

When hunting, the jaguar lies flat and unmoving on a low branch. If a tapir, hog, or deer passes beneath the tree, the jaguar pounces and digs in its claws. Its very strong teeth can slice through bone!

Which is the slowest mammal in the rain forest?

The three-toed sloth. Sloths take their time doing everything. Hanging upside down from a tree branch, they slowly eat the leaves. At the rate a sloth moves, it takes about 10 hours to travel 1 mile (1.6 km). It can take a whole month to digest a meal!

Sloths are so slow, in fact, that plantlike algae grow in their fur. The greenish color of the algae makes sloths hard to see, protecting them from hungry predators.

About once a week a sloth slowly lowers itself to the floor of the forest. The animal deposits its waste on the ground. Then it goes back to hanging upside down in the canopy. The wastes enrich the soil and help plants to grow.

How do some snakes find their prey in the dark?

With special heat sensors. The sensors let them detect the heat given off by other animals. The fer-de-lance, a snake that lives on the ground, hides among leaf litter, tree roots, and buttresses. Little holes in its head, called pit organs, are highly sensitive to heat, helping the snake track and catch warm-blooded animals in the dark.

Another snake, the emerald tree boa, coils up on a branch, waiting for its next meal to pass by. The snake can sense even the smallest change in temperature. This lets it locate its prey. When an animal comes near, the boa strikes, seizing the victim and squeezing it tighter and tighter until it is dead. For big prey, the snake's jaws stretch wide open to swallow the animal in one huge gulp!

Emerald tree boa

Jaguar

Which is the most poisonous frog in the rain forest?

The poison arrow frog. This small frog is no longer than your thumb and very colorful. Its bright hues warn predators to stay away.

The frog's poison is strong enough to kill an animal in seconds. Hunters who live in the Amazon rain forest use it on the tips of their arrows.

How many kinds of insects live in the rain forest?

As many as 80 million. This includes ants, bees, butterflies, beetles, moths, and mosquitoes. In fact, the rain forest is home to more than 240 species of army ants alone!

Army ants

How did army ants get their name?

From the way they march. Army ants seem to be following commands, like troops following a general into battle. Sometimes they move in one big mass, as if ready to launch a full-scale frontal attack. Other times they form long, narrow lines. This makes them look like they are trying to surround the enemy. Either way, the sight and rustling sound of army ants on the march will chill your bones!

Which ants grow food on leaf mush?

Leaf-cutter ants. The ants climb tree trunks in single file and cut off pieces of leaves with their sharp jaws. Holding the pieces over their heads like umbrellas, they march back to their underground nests. They chew the plant parts into a wet pulp. In time, fungus grows on the mush. The fungus is the only food that these ants eat.

Leaf-cutter ants

Passionflower
butterflies

Caterpillar

How do some insects avoid enemies?

They use camouflage. On the dim forest floor, a katydid looks just like a fallen leaf. One type of praying mantis resembles the petals of an orchid. And the caterpillar of the swallowtail butterfly looks just like a fresh bird dropping—a sickening disguise that fools hungry predators.

Are any butterflies poisonous?

Yes, some are. In its caterpillar stage, the passionflower butterfly eats the leaves of the poisonous passionflower—and the toxin stays in its body. Its bright colors warn away would-be predators.

Which are the most harmful insects in the tropical rain forest?

Botflies. These bloodsucking flies lay eggs on mammals, including humans. When the eggs hatch, the larvae burrow under the skin. They eat the flesh, which may result in death.

Which are the most feared fish of the rain forest?

Piranhas. Piranhas swim in rain forest rivers, like the Amazon, and in lakes. Among the 5,000 different kinds of fish in the rain forest, piranhas have the biggest appetites. These small, fierce animals use their razor-sharp teeth to rip apart their prey. Piranhas hunt fish and other water creatures, but they seldom attack people.

Which animal is not afraid of piranhas?

The Amazon river dolphin. Cotton-candy pink in color, these river dolphins prey on the ferocious piranhas. The dolphins' long snouts and broad flippers help them catch the piranhas in the dark, murky river waters of South America's rain forest.

Do fish climb trees in the rain forest?

In a way, yes. Many tropical rain forests are flooded for several months a year. The river water often rises as high as 45 feet (14 m), reaching up to the tree branches. So-called tree-climbing fish swim among the branches, eating seeds and catching insects on the leaves and bark. Special eyes let the fish see both underwater and in the air.

Which reptiles live in rain forest rivers?

Crocodiles, among others. These reptiles often lie in shallow water looking like sunken logs. Here they await their next meal of fish, birds, or turtles. If you look carefully, you may spot a basilisk lizard scooting on top of the water. Its speed and big rear feet keep it from sinking!

Amazon river dolphins

Piranhas

PEOPLE IN THE RAIN FOREST

How many people live in tropical rain forests?

About 200 million. Most indigenous, or native, rain forest people live in small groups. Some indigenous people get most of their food, medicine, clothing, and shelter by hunting animals and gathering wild plants in the rain forest. Others grow crops on small farms. Still others work outside their communities, logging, mining, exploring for oil, or raising cattle. For many people who live in rain forests, ways of life are rapidly changing.

Are there cities in rain forests?

Not now. But between 1,750 and 1,000 years ago, a group of people called the Maya built a number of cities in the tropical rain forests of Mexico and Central America. Some of the cities had 100,000 or more inhabitants. Skilled builders, painters, and sculptors, the Maya had an advanced system of writing, as well as a good understanding of mathematics and astronomy.

Around the same time, another group of people built the magnificent city of Angkor in the rain forest of present-day Cambodia. One of the wonders of the ancient world, Angkor covered 40 square miles (104 km^2) and was home to about two million people.

What happened to these ancient cities?

People abandoned them. Over the centuries, the buildings fell into ruin and the forests grew over the remains. Today, scientists study the sites of these old cities. The forests still have not returned to their original state. The lesson is clear. Once sections of the rain forest are destroyed, they may be gone forever.

A temple in the ancient city of Angkor

An Efe camp in the Democratic Republic of Congo

Which rain forest people hunt animals and gather plants?

The Penan of Borneo, the Agta of the Philippines, and the Efe and Mbuti (mm-BOO-tee) of the Democratic Republic of Congo, among others. These people usually live together in small groups, moving from place to place when food becomes scarce. Their impact on the forest is tiny because their numbers are few and they don't stay in any one place for very long.

Do people that live in the rain forest usually hunt in large groups?

No. Yanomami men in Brazil, for example, hunt alone or in groups of two or three. They use weapons, such as large blowpipes or bows and poison-tipped arrows. Small groups of Mbuti men usually go into the forest with large nets made of forest vines. The women and children then bang on drums and tree trunks to scare animals, such as the small, deerlike duikers (DYE-kerz), into the semicircle of nets held by the men. The men kill the animals they catch and divide up the meat.

Which foods do people gather from the rain forest?

Wild nuts, berries, mushrooms, roots, and fruit. Yanomami women roast or boil bananas and plantains or make them into soup. They also dry and grate a root of the cassava plant, called manioc, which they use to make flat, round bread.

How do Mbuti people find honey?

With the help of a bird called a honeyguide. The honeyguide likes to eat beeswax, but its beak is not strong enough to break into the hive. So the birds have learned to lead Mbuti people to the hive.

The bird flies ahead, wildly chattering and waving its white tail feathers. Upon arrival, the people hack open the hive, remove the honey—and leave the beeswax for the honeyguide!

How do indigenous farmers prepare their fields?

By a method known as "slash and burn." The farmers cut down the trees in a small patch and burn the debris to clear the field. The ash left by the fire makes a nutrient-rich bed for crops that lasts a few years. In the rich soil, the farmers grow dozens of kinds of plants, including corn, bananas, sweet potatoes, tomatoes, peanuts, avocados, and papaya. When a field loses its fertility, the farmers clear another patch of forest, leaving the forest to grow back in the older plot.

Some settlers from outside the rain forest slash and burn huge tracts of land. Such large-scale destruction of the forest leaves little chance that these areas will ever grow back.

Do rain forest farmers sell their crops?

Not usually. Native rain forest farmers generally live in villages with several other families. They cultivate small plots near their homes and grow just enough to feed relatives and others in the community, or to trade for other products.

What are shamans?

Doctors or medicine people. Shamans have learned how to use wild plants to treat human diseases. From shamans have come hundreds of drugs now used by doctors throughout the world. Rain forest shamans still have much to teach us.

Yanomami people planting manioc in an area that has been cleared using the slash-and-burn method

What is happening to the rain forest?

It is being destroyed. Every day, workers clear about 96,000 acres (38,842 ha) of land for farms, ranches, gold mines, and oil wells.

In the year 1800, rain forests formed an almost unbroken green belt through tropical North and South America, Africa, Asia, and Australia. They covered about 20 percent of Earth's land surface. Today, rain forests are broken up into a series of small green pockets that cover less than 7 percent of the planet.

What happens to plants, animals, and people as rain forests disappear?

Thousands of species of plants and animals become extinct. Thus far, scientists have studied only a small percentage of the millions of plants and animals that live in tropical rain forests. As they disappear, we lose the promise of any number of helpful new medicines, foods, and other products.

Native peoples die at a young age of disease or are forced to abandon land that they and their ancestors have lived on for centuries. In recent times, the population of indigenous people in the Amazon rain forest has plummeted from an estimated 9 million to fewer than 200,000. Without these peoples, the world loses a priceless understanding and knowledge of the rain forest. Gone, too, are their cultures and traditions.

How can we protect the rain forest?

We can join organizations that are working to save the rain forests and help the native people that live there. We can write to government officials, asking them to pass laws protecting the world's rain forests. We can help others understand the importance of the world's rain forests. We can stop buying products made from rain forest woods. And we can stop eating hamburgers made from cattle raised on cleared rain forest land.

The rain forest has evolved gradually over millions of years. Let's do all we can to protect, study, and appreciate this amazing natural world.

Scarlet macaw

Two-toed sloth

Amazon parrot

INDEX

About the Authors

In writing this book, the Bergers drew on two firsthand experiences: sailing up and down the Amazon River and visiting settlements and villages in the Brazilian rain forest along the way. "We hope that our readers will help spread the word about the need to protect this precious resource," they say.

About the Illustrator

Michael Rothman has been interested in tropical biology since he was a child. As part of his work as an illustrator, he has traveled to the rain forests of French Guiana with scientists from the New York Botanical Garden. While in French Guiana, he learned how to climb trees up into the canopy using spikes.